Stories from the Shepherd's heart

Stories about sheep to delight both the young and the old readers

Nancy Yonker

Follow The Shepherd
Nancy

Copyright © 2010 by Nancy Yonker

Stories from the Shepherd's heart
by Nancy Yonker

Printed in the United States of America

ISBN 9781615796588

All rights reserved solely by the author. The author guarantees all contents are original and do not infringe upon the legal rights of any other person or work. No part of this book may be reproduced in any form without the permission of the author. The views expressed in this book are not necessarily those of the publisher.

Unless otherwise indicated, Bible quotations are taken from the New International version of the Bible. Copyright © 1974 by Zondervan Bible Publishers in Grand Rapids, MI.

www.xulonpress.com

Table of Contents

1. Preview...ix
2. Lambs... 11
3. Frosty 18
4. Freedom 21
5. Sheep Shearing...25
6. Simon 30
7. A Tribute to Loretta..35
8. Danger on the Sheep Farm...39
9. Adoption 43
10. Orphan Anne 48
11. A Good Laugh on the Sheep Farm 53
12. Shepherds and Sheep...56
13. The Sound of the trumpet..59
14. Lessons From the Good Shepherd 63

The shepherd's stories are in memory
of our daughter, Rachel Ann who died of leukemia at age 7.
She is safe with Jesus waiting for us.

The shepherd would also like to dedicate the stories
to our 14 grandchildren, so they can all know
The Good Shepherd.

Sarah
Laura
Carrie
Alexandra
Andrew
Solomon
Victoria
Nathan John
Rachel
Nikolas
Ekaterina
Heather
Hannah
Caleb

Preview

The Lord is my Shepherd. I shall lack nothing. He is beautiful beyond description! My Shepherd supplies everything I need, everything I need to live or die by.

I am compelled to write my story; I cannot keep silent. I have heard too often that sheep are "dumb". I write not only to defend sheep, but also to show how God compares us to sheep. God is our Shepherd and we are His sheep.

My love affair with sheep began many years ago when we bought two lambs as pets for our children. Since then, we have always kept a few sheep.

Sheep have taught our family many lessons. I think of my relationship to the sheep and understand better my relationship to God.

Over and over again, God calls His people sheep. While caring for sheep, I'm often reminded of the following verses: *"My sheep listen to my voice; I know them and they follow me."* (John 10a:27) *"He tends his flock like a shepherd: He gathers the lambs in His arms and carries them close to His heart; he gently leads those that have young."* (Isaiah 40:11) *"The Lord is my Shepherd. I shall lack nothing."*

(Psalm 23:1) **"You, my sheep, the sheep of my pasture, are people, and I am your God, declares the Sovereign Lord."** (Ezekiel 34:31) *"The mountains skipped like Rams, the hills like sheep."* (Psalm 114:4)

I also think of the beautiful parable of Jesus searching for the one lost sheep. After all, there were ninety-nine sheep safe in the fold, but he cared about that one. When he found it, the angels rejoiced in heaven. In Revelation we see God, the Great Judge, separating the sheep from the goats.

Would God compare us to something so degrading and stupid? We, His sheep are made in His image.

Do we need our Shepherd to guide us safely through life? Absolutely! Are we, like sheep, totally dependent on our Shepherd? Yes, Yes, Yes!

Even Jesus is pictured as a lamb, a sacrificial lamb. Jesus took our place, took our sin. I'm so happy to be a sheep of His flock.

Lambs

Little lambs are born anytime between December and June. They come in all colors: white, black, brown, and spotted and some have white bodies with black faces and feet. Sometimes mother sheep have one baby. Sometimes they have twins or they even have triplets! Little boy lambs are called rams and little girl lambs are called ewes.

Sheep farmers, who are called shepherds, are very busy when the time for lambs to be born has come. They have to get up in the middle of the night to check on mother sheep to be sure they are all right. They don't want mother sheep to have any problems. Usually the shepherd can help the mother sheep so the lambs can be born safely. The pens have to be kept clean and the mother sheep needs a pen all by herself so the other big sheep will not accidentally step on her new babies. The shepherd is especially watchful on a cold winter night. New lambs cannot take the cold, drafty, winter winds. They would get a bad cold just like you do in the wintertime.

For some strange reason, little lambs love to be born on the coldest day of the year. Then they shiver in the cold and the shepherd gently wraps them in a blanket and warms them and dries them off.

Sometimes when lambs are born they are very weak and the shepherd helps them. He shows them where to find their mother's warm milk and occasionally even gets them started with a bottle of warm milk.

Usually, right after the lambs are born, they lie very quietly for awhile; then, with the urging of mother sheep, they try to stand on their feet. Their legs are so long and weak! They wobble and wobble and fall flat on their stomachs! Some lambs are born stronger than others, They are born crying for food! Mother sheep loves her babies very much. It usually does not matter to her if she has one, two, or three.

She cleans them all up and gently nudges them to where the warm milk is. She talks to them all the while. That is called nickering.

The babies are so precious and soft and woolly. You just want to hold and cuddle them all the time, but this makes mother sheep very nervous. She cries for her babies and wants you to put them back in her pen.

Mother sheep is very careful with her new babies. Because the night is very dark and she is large and the lambs are small, she does want to step on them or lie on them.

All of the little lambs are given names, sometimes according to their personality. The shepherd calls his sheep and lambs by name just as our Good Shepherd calls us by name. John 10:3 says, "He (Jesus) calls His own sheep by name and leads them out."

Baby lambs need shots and vaccinations just like you do. When the lambs are about a week old, the shepherd has to cut off their long tail. Mr. Shepherd does not want to hurt his lambs, but their tail is very bothersome to them and it gets in their way and becomes dirty and collects flies. By the time the lambs are two or three weeks old, they are very lively and are becoming strong. They can easily squeeze through the holes in their mothers' pens. If there is only one lamb, it usually is more shy and stays closer to its mother, but when there are two lambs, they are more daring and become naughty! They run away from their mother. Mother sheep stamps her feet and bellows loudly, but they do not listen. They scamper away – they are very curious and very friendly.

They check out the big barn, play with the kittens, chase the ducks, get into the shepherd's hay, and nibble on the shepherd's pant legs when he is busy doing something. They run out of the barn and eat the new spring flowers. When they realize they are a long way from their mother, they turn and jump three feet in the air and run as fast as they can back to their pen, kicking up their heels all the way.

The shepherd has several pens with mothers in them who are waiting for their lambs to be born. That way, the shepherd can take special care of these mothers. The little lambs, already born, always peer into these pens – waiting for the big event – waiting to coax the new lambs to come out of their pens so they can play together. What fun little lambs have together!

Did you know lambs have friends just like you do? They even have best friends. The little lambs run outside together and investigate everything. Sometimes when they skip back to the barn, they accidentally run into the wrong pen! The strange mother butts the little lamb and lets him know he does not belong to her. "Ouch! Mama, where are you?"

Every afternoon, lambs and mothers take a nap just like children do. If you could come into the big barn, you would see the little lambs lying on their mother's back. It looks so funny.

The mother and babies stay penned up for about a month. That gives the mother a chance to rest and the lambs a chance to grow strong. After that, they go into the big pen. They join their father and the mothers who already had their lambs. Now they can go into the big pasture.

The first few hours are utter confusion. The mothers fight together. They back up and then come forward with all their force and bang heads together. They must get an awful headache! The lambs watch and then begin to fight with the other lambs.

After awhile they all settle down. They begin to accept each other and, once again, enjoy their daily lives.

All the little lambs now begin to run together; they love to feel the freedom of the big pasture. They love to run away from their mothers; they feel independent. They play hide and seek. They hide and mother sheep comes seeking them, crying all the time. They also play tag. All the while, they jump three feet off the ground and skip. They also love to have fun in a strange manner – they lift all four feet off the ground and run. Thump – thump – hop – hop.

By the time the lambs are a year old, they are almost full grown and ready to have babies on their own.

Stories from the Shepherd's heart

Stories from the Shepherd's heart

Stories from the Shepherd's heart

Frosty

The cold winter winds had been blowing all night. When morning came on that cold, four-below- zero January morning, the shepherd went out to check his sheep. He brought them hay and corn and fresh water. He turned to go back to the warm fire of the large country kitchen, but something caught his attention . . . One of the sheep stayed near the door, almost as though she was afraid to come in and eat. The shepherd looked outside the door and there, to his utter surprise, lay a small white lamb, nearly frozen to death. The shepherd could see she was alive, but she was already stiff and cold and covered with frosty snow. The shepherd knew he had to act quickly to save the life of this baby, born out in the cold.

    He gently picked her up and carried her in his arms to the warm country kitchen. He remembered his own shepherd, the Lord Jesus, Who "gathers the lambs in His arms and carries them close to His heart." Isaiah 40:11.

    The shepherd gently wrapped the little white lamb in a blanket and laid her near the warm wood stove, her little body beginning to shiver. The shepherd prepared a warm bottle of rich milk for her. He tried to get her to suck, just a little at a time. The shepherd did all he could, but was afraid the little lamb became to chilled and would surely die.

After a few hours, to the amazement of the shepherd, the lamb stood on her wobbly feet and cried, "Baa-aaa", a weak but happy sound to the shepherd's ears.

The shepherd brought the little white lamb, whom he lovingly called "Frosty", back to her mother in the barn. By now, too much time had gone by and the mother became nervous and would not take care of her baby.

The cold January winds did not show signs of letting up, and the big barn was too cold for a new lamb without the care of mother sheep. The shepherd brought Frosty back to the warmth of the country kitchen, and there he kept Frosty in a big box filled with straw. She was now an orphan lamb.

The cold winter lasted longer than normal, and Frosty lived in her big box in the shepherd's kitchen for six weeks. Every four hours, the shepherd would give Frosty a bottle of warm milk. Little lambs have to be taken care of much the same way as human babies. They even drink their warm milk from a regular baby bottle! Frosty even woke her shepherd up in the middle of the night! After she would drink her bottle of warm rich milk, she would sleep like a baby until morning.

Frosty grew and became too big for her box. It was now the middle of March. The warmer spring breezes were beginning to blow, and the sun was becoming warm. The crocuses were pushing their way through the ground. The shepherd knew Frosty had to go back to the barn with the other sheep.

It was not easy for Frosty. She did not like the other sheep. She did not like the barn smells. She did not want the shepherd to leave her alone. She was used to living with people; she felt closer to people than to sheep. The shepherd understood her problem and made her a little pen by herself, and when he was outside to watch her, he let her run freely. She would run out of the barn and back to the house. There she would paste her little face against the kitchen door and pitifully cry, "Baa-aa".

It took time for her to learn to associate with the other sheep, but she always loved her shepherd the best. No matter where she would be in the big pasture, when the shepherd called "Frosty", she would come to him. She never forgot her shepherd's kindness to her. When he is outside, she follows him. She rewards her kind shepherd with twin lambs every spring and is a good mother.

"I am the good shepherd; I know my sheep and my sheep know me." John 10:14

Freedom

It was a cold mid-winter morning. The shepherd on the happy sheep farm lay down to sleep. You see, the shepherd had worked all night and was exhausted. The bed was warm and inviting. The quilts were so warm and comforting. The shepherd snuggled deep inside them, and within minutes was in a deep, restful slumber.

I've said this so many times before; I have to say it again. I am so glad my Shepherd is the eternal all-knowing, all-seeing, never-sleeping God; I am always in His care. Human shepherds have shortcomings; they get tired, they are in a unconscious state in sleep.

The shepherd on the happy sheep farm was not aware of any of the events which happened on that cold morning. Someone on the happy sheep farm left the gate open to the sheep pen and this enabled the sheep to roam as they so pleased.

The shepherd was awakened by loud knocking on the window. He could hardly get his wits together. Grumbling, he got up – how could anyone be so inconsiderate as to interrupt his sleep like that? He grabbed a coat and went outside.

The sheep had filed one by one through the open gate, getting themselves into nothing but trouble. They stripped all the Indian corn bare and left empty bunches of corn all over the sheep farm. They pulled apart the beautiful broom stick corn stalks, of which the shepherd was so proud. They trampled it down and its beauty lay in a heap at their feet.

When there wasn't anything more exciting to do in the yard, they placed themselves in grave danger outside of the shepherd's watchful eye. It was told to the shepherd later that the whole flock had entertained themselves in the middle of the busy road. Without their shepherd, they did not know they were in danger!

One good Samaritan stopped and herded the sheep back into the barn, but he was unaware that the gate was open. He knocked and knocked on the shepherd's door, but the shepherd was enjoying a deep sleep.

The sheep, once again, filed through the open gate and slowly wandered back to the road. Another good Samaritan herded them off the road. She coaxed them to the barn with an ear of corn that had been stuck in he tree for the birds. This time, the sheep leaped one by one over the fence – even the old sheep of the flock who was stiff, normally – even the mothers with their big bellies full of lambs yet to be born. This good Samaritan also failed to see the open gate. She could not awaken the shepherd either.

One more time the sheep filed on by one through the open gate. This time they made a turn and visited neighbors. By now the neighborhood was drawn into the excitement. Where was the shepherd? Phones began to ring, but they could not arouse the sleeping shepherd.

The neighbors joined forces and herded the flock back home again. They spotted the open gate and the sheep lost their freedom. The neighbors knew the shepherd well, and it was one of them who awoke the shepherd by pounding on his bedroom window!

The shepherd went into the barn to check the situation. The sheep looked so innocent. Big, brown eyes filled with love were looking at the shepherd. It was hard for him to imagine all the trouble these sheep had gotten themselves into, but the mess they made was evident all over the place. The shepherd loved them, in spite of the trouble they caused.

The shepherd mused while enjoying a cup of hot coffee. He had to think of his Good Shepherd, who cannot make mistakes. He thought about, His sheep, who sometimes willfully leave His fold; we too, unknown to us, fall into serious danger – away from Christian fellowship and love. We think we have found freedom, but it is only the devil's lie. Praise God, our Good Shepherd sends good Samaritans to our rescue. They talk to us, encourage us, love us and pray for us. They ever lead us, by God's word, back into the fold, the only place where true freedom and safety dwell.

The human shepherd needed help. And our Heavenly Father, the Good Shepherd, uses people to bring the lost to Himself. Praise God! When we return to the fold, God looks at us, loves us, forgives us, and wraps around us His arms of love and protection.

Stories from the Shepherd's heart

Sheep Shearing

Springtime at the sheep farm is a very busy time. The shepherd spends a lot of sleepless nights caring for mother sheep as her little lambs are born. There is another big event which happens every spring at the sheep farm. It is called sheep shearing. When the very first hints of spring arrive, the shepherd remembers that it is time for the sheep to get rid of their warm winter coats.

Sheep shearing is hard work. First, the shepherd has to make sure all the sheep are locked up in the big barn. The sheep shearers do not want to shear the sheep's wool if it is wet. Once the sheep are able to run outside, they are hard to convince to come back in.

On the morning of sheep shearing, the shepherd makes a light, airy spot ready in the big barn, or outside, where there is plenty of room to shear the sheep.

Soon the big truck of the sheep shearers arrives and backs up to the barn. Out come the big burlap sacks for the wool, then the scale to weigh the wool once it is sheared, then the big mat to lay the sheep on and finally, the large razor to separate the wool from the sheep.

The sheep shearers are strong, ruddy looking men. Their work is hard and back-breaking. A good sheep shearer can handle a sheep all by himself while shearing.

After a hot cup of coffee, the men are ready to get on with their work.

Only the adult sheep get sheared; lambs will wait their turn until the following spring. The shepherd now goes and brings out the sheep, one at a time, to the sheep shearers. First of all, the shepherd likes to get the ram (father sheep). He is the biggest, strongest sheep of the flock. He is usually very hard to handle – stubborn and sometimes even a little mean. The shepherd needs help with him. The two men corner him and drag him to the mat. They have to wrestle him to the ground as he is as strong as the two men. Once they have him laying on his side, the battle is over. He may kick a little and try to get up, but the two men can now easily handle him.

Sheep do not utter a sound while being sheared. Isaiah 53:7 compares Jesus, who did not open his mouth when being led away to be crucified, to a sheep who is silent before her shearers.

The rams usually have the most beautiful, warmest coat. The shearers start at the top of the head and, with their big razor, trim away the warm coat from the sheep's body. The coat is thick. On the outside it looks dirty but underneath it is soft and clean and beautiful. The shearers do beautiful work. The wool comes off in one big piece; it does not hurt the sheep at all. It is like you getting a haircut.

When the shearer is done, he takes the sheep's old winter coat and stuffs it into a big burlap sack. Now the big old ram feels naked and embarrassed and cold, but he is clean and does not smell anymore. He looks smaller and is much easier to handle. The shepherd drags him to the pasture and returns for another sheep from the big barn.

One by one the ewes, or mother sheep, get sheared. They are more gentle than the ram and much easier to handle. Their coat, too, is good and beautiful but not as heavy as the ram's. So many of the ewe's nutrients from their food go into producing healthy babies and milk to feed their babies; their wool gets the nutrients last of all. That is why the shepherd takes special care to tend well to the mother sheep. I can't help but think of Isaiah 40:11.

> "Jesus tends His flock like a shepherd.
> He gathers the lambs in His arms
> and carries them close to His heart;
> He gently leads those that have young."

The shepherd always is amazed at sheep-shearing time at the marvelous way God made sheep and lambs and wool, and about the sheep's nature. The shepherd always remembers that God compared him to those sheep. The shepherd, too, is dependent on His great Shepherd – Jesus Christ.

While mother sheep is being sheared, her lambs are frantic. The shepherd tries to keep them away from their mother, but sometimes it is impossible. The lambs cannot understand why mama sheep is laying down. Why are the men working on her? Is she sick? Will she die? That awful noise of the big razor! And then when the sheep shearer is done shearing mother sheep, something awful has happened. She lost her coat. Every mother sheep has a certain smell on that coat and the lambs use that smell to identify their own mother. When the coat is sheared off, the lambs no longer can identify their mother by smelling her.

The shepherd takes mother sheep to the pasture, but the lambs will no longer follow her. The shepherd's wife gathers the lambs in her arms and gently carries them to their mother. Mother sheep

calls to her babies, but they no longer know her. They cry and cry and run frantically around the pasture. Mother runs to them and they run away in fear. Mother sheep knows her babies but they do not know her. Sometimes you can hear the pathetic cry of baby lambs for twenty-four hours after shearing. Finally, due to hunger and the constant urging of the mother, baby and mother are once again bonded together.

It took all afternoon, but the men are finally done. All the wool is packed into burlap sacks. The black wool is separated from the white wool. The wool is then weighed.

After that, the wool is cleaned and separated into long cords and woven together for yarn and wool material for warm blankets and sweaters and coats and skirts. Just think! The warm coat you wear in wintertime to keep you warm could have been worn by sheep in winters before!

God knew man would be cold and would need warm blankets and coats. In His great wisdom, He created sheep to provide us with the warm things we need!

Stories from the Shepherd's heart

Simon

The shepherd could see Simon was going to make a very good ram. A ram, you now know, is a father sheep. The shepherd was feeding his sheep in the big barn when he found Simon. Simon was probably an hour old, but he was already standing on his feet strongly. He looked confident, sure of himself, and you could easily see he had found his mother's warm milk all by himself. He was a beauty! White body, black face, black legs. The shepherd knew he would be a leader.

Simon grew fast. He had his mother's warm milk all to himself; he didn't have to share with a twin.

Simon loved his mother, but he always loved to scamper away to investigate life. He knew every corner of the big barn and he loved the big outdoors. You could often see Simon poking his head into the pens where the other mother sheep were and hoping for new lambs to play with. When he found them he coaxed them to come out and play. The shepherd could always see lambs skipping and jumping with Simon in the lead.

Simon was bold, unafraid, and very playful. He loved to kick his feet at the kittens and then he would stare at them until they pawed at his nose. He loved to nibble on the shepherd's clothes as they were hanging outside to dry.

Simon saw spring come with its warm, gentle breezes and warm spring rains. The flowers were waking up from their long winter naps. They poked their heads out of the warm, moist ground and sleepily said, "Good morning, merry sunshine!" Simon took a real liking to those tender little spring flowers, and the shepherd knew it was time to pen Simon up into the big pasture. There he could roam without getting into so much trouble.

How Simon loved the big pasture! The grass was lush and green, and the lambs ran and skipped and jumped and played games together. When they wandered too far from their mother, the mother sheep bellowed until they came back. Every afternoon Simon and his mother laid in the shade of the big oak tree and took a nap.

It did not take Simon very long to investigate every inch of the big pasture. He was becoming bored, and he decided he would like to know what was on the other side of the fence. One day Simon, found a hole in the fence just big enough for his head to fit through. He didn't mind. The grass tasted so good on the other side! He soon had eaten enough and heard his mother calling him to follow her, but try as hard as could, his head was stuck in the fence and he could not get it out! He pulled and pulled, and cried and cried. The afternoon sun beat down upon him, but just when he was ready to give up, he saw the shepherd coming to help him.

Stories from the Shepherd's heart

It cured Simon for awhile. He stayed close to his mother in the big pasture. Now summer had come. It was a long time ago that Simon's head had been caught. Simon was now much stronger. His body was becoming husky. He was strong and healthy. He hardly needed his mother's care anymore.

The sheep were grazing in the pasture as far back as they could go; the big barn was hidden from their view. Simon once again longed to know what was on the other side of the fence. Simon backed up and ran forward and leaped through the air, like a deer, over the fence. It seemed so easy to him. It was fun! No one seemed to miss him, not even his mother; but then, he rarely stayed near her anymore. The grass was greener just like it had seemed to him. It wasn't trodden down at all.

The bluejays screeched at Simon; they knew he was not where he belonged. Simon didn't pay any attention to them. As he was eating, he was wandering farther and farther away. A bunny scurried across his path, surprised so see Simon in his territory. Simon was enjoying himself so much. He wandered over to a clump of long grass, and startled a fawn waiting for her mother to return.

Simon was having fun! He wandered through the lush grass, through the trees, and into the clearing where the farmer grew pumpkins. They were young and tender, and oh, how good they tasted. It was not until his stomach was so full that if felt like it would burst, that Simon realized how lost he was. He looked all around but could not see the big pasture.

By now the other sheep had returned to the big barn. The older sheep knew night was coming and they desired to be in a place of safety.

Stories from the Shepherd's heart

As Simon was searching for the big pasture, he was instead wandering farther away. He had never been so scared in all of his young life. He was so alone. The darkness was falling and he heard so many strange noises. Oh, what was that? A flash of lightning! A storm was coming!

How Simon wished he had stayed in the big pasture. He thought about the big barn; he was so thirsty. He felt he would die out there all alone. He cried, "baa-baaaa, ma-maaa".

The shepherd knew a storm was coming – the day had been hot and sticky. He wanted to make sure his flock was safe. He knew they would like a cool drink of water. As he was lovingly gathering the sheep to the water, he missed Simon. The shepherd left the other sheep and quickly searched the big pasture. No sign of Simon. Darkness was beginning to fall, and in the distance, he could hear thunder.

The shepherd got his lantern and searched in the darkness for Simon. The ground was uneven and low branches whipped him in the face. He stumbled, calling out, "Simon, Simon!" The thunder seemed to be coming closer and he now saw lightening. The shepherd reached the pumpkin patch, ever stumbling forward in the darkness. He made his way slowly to the neighbor's field, thick with tall weeds, always calling out, "Simon!"

Simon's little heart leaped for joy – he heard his shepherd's voice calling him. A weak little "baa" came from his voice. The shepherd shone his lantern close to the ground and there lay Simon – so alone and tired and thirsty and afraid . The shepherd gently picked him up and placed him on his shoulders and carefully stepped through the darkness toward home.

Stories from the Shepherd's heart

    The lightning was brighter, the thunder was louder, and it was now raining. The shepherd did not mind. He had found his lost lamb.

    Simon was soon in the safety of the big barn. How happy he was. He loved his shepherd and knew he never wanted to wander again.

    Did you know that sometimes we are tempted to leave the safety of a Christian life? We think our parents are old-fashioned. We imagine we could have a lot more fun out in the world. Then we make a wrong decision and leave our father's home. We soon learn that the world just is not as much fun as we thought it would be. People who do not love Jesus <u>really</u> do not care about us; Satan is no friend of ours. We become lost and alone and lonely – just like Simon. We are all mixed up and cannot seem to find our way back. We are just like poor, wandering sheep.

    Our great Shepherd, Jesus, always loves us and sees us in our lost condition. He always cares and He comes seeking us. When He finds us, He carries us back to the place of safety – back to the Shepherd's fold. Guess what? Even the angels in heaven see us return and they rejoice!

    In Luke 15:4-7. Jesus Himself tells us a story about lost sheep. We are the sheep in the story, lost, wandering, away from God, alone, lonely. The Good Shepherd , who is Jesus, seeks us, finds us, and carries us home. The angels rejoice because we are safe in the family of God!

A Tribute to Loretta

The shepherd calls gently to Loretta. Slowly she gets up on her feet; she now has arthritis and cannot move very fast anymore. She makes her way to the fence, awaiting the gentle pat on her head from her shepherd. Loretta has already lived years past the life span of a sheep. She cannot keep up with the younger sheep; they ignore her anyway, not understanding how she feels. So she spends her days mostly alone, near the safety of the barn.

The shepherd fondly remembers many years before when, entering the barn one cold February morning to feed his sheep, there was Loretta, anxiously waiting for him to come so she could show off her new twins! What a mother Loretta was; there was no other ewe quite like her – totally devoted to her babies! Her little twins could never get out of her sight.

The shepherd will never forget the February, a week later, when Loretta got into something by mistake (something never intended for a sheep to consume). She became deathly sick. She lay near death for ten days. She couldn't stand, and her stomach was bloated. The vet came every day, but shook his head sadly, and gave little or no hope for her recovery. Loretta watched with sad eyes. The shepherd bottle-fed the twins, but kept them with Loretta. They lay close to her, sometimes on her back and sometimes near her head, keeping their mother from giving up completely.

Every two hours, day and night, the shepherd slipped a little cod liver oil, raw egg, milk, and sugar into her mouth, forcing her to swallow. The shepherd would put little bits of hay in her mouth, always encouraging her to fight back. The vet shook his head, wondering if it was worth it all, but he knew in his heart that the only way Loretta could pull through was because of the great love the shepherd was showing.

After ten long days, a miracle happened! With the shepherd's help Loretta stood on her wobbly feet! Not for long – only a minute – then she plopped down again, but the shepherd knew Loretta was fighting and she would make it. The shepherd had been praying for Loretta every day, and he was overjoyed. All his hard work and sleepless nights were now worth it all.

It wasn't long after that Loretta was again able to stand on her own, and if you think the shepherd had great joy, you should have seen the twins! They never forgot Loretta or her warm milk or her gentle nudging, and Loretta never forgot her babies! Then a second miracle happened. One morning when the shepherd came into the barn, the twins were again nursing from Loretta!

It is now one of the fondest memories the shepherd has from his sheep.

Loretta is old now; some would say useless. But she will remain with good care until her time has come.

If a human shepherd can love so much, can you even begin to imagine how much our Good Shepherd loves us? He is here all our lives long. Our Shepherd is here comforting, healing, encouraging and, pulling us through the hard times.

In old age, when some think our usefulness to society has ceased, our Good Shepherd is busy making that home ready for us. He is there comforting us in the lonely hours, reassuring us, and sticking closer to us than a brother.

Never neglect the old sheep of the flock. They belong to the Shepherd and He loves them. They have served their Shepherd all their lives and they now deserve our deep respect and love.

As with Loretta, let's care for them until the Good Shepherd calls them home!

> The Lord is my shepherd,
> I shall lack nothing.
> He makes me lie down in
> green pastures;
> He leads me beside quiet waters.
> He restores my soul;
> He guides me in paths of righteousness
> for His name's sake.
> Even though I walk through
> the valley of the shadow of death,
> I will fear no evil;
> for you are with me;
> Your rod and your staff,
> they comfort me;
> you prepare a table before me

in the presence of my enemies;
You anoint my head with oil;
My cup overflows.
Surely goodness and love will
follow me all the days of my life,
And I will dwell in the house
of the Lord <u>forever</u>.
      Psalm 23

Praise His name!

Danger on the Sheep Farm

The shepherd wishes there was never a sad story to tell. The shepherd would always like the pasture to be a place of happiness and safety; but because many years ago sin entered the world, man and animals, in fact the whole creation, is suffering today. Romans 8:22 states that "even the earth groans because of sin."

It wasn't always that way. God created the most beautiful world you could ever imagine. Just think about a place which sin had never touched. Everything was in harmony. The animals got along together, there was no pain, no thorns, no fighting – just perfect beauty everywhere.

Then sin came into the picture. We all know the story about Adam and Eve, the Garden of Eden, and the serpent. Everything changed. Man began to hate his brother. He was afraid of God. He began to lie and steal, he became greedy. He loved himself more than others. The beautiful earth suffered too. Weeds and thorns grew in the beautiful garden; things began to rot and die. There was sickness and pain. The animals no longer were friends. They became wild and mean; they were afraid of each other and man.

Because of all these things, problems come on the sheep farm. The pasture is not always happy. The shepherd watches his flock closely, but also imperfectly. In Bible times the shepherd lived with his sheep, but that is not done so much anymore today. In the story about the shepherds and the angels at the time of Jesus' birth, the Bible says, "The shepherds were living out in the field, keeping watch over their flock by night." (Luke 2:8)

One night on the sheep farm, while the shepherd was sleeping, four large German Shepherd dogs, left to roam, killed all the shepherd's sheep except two. One sheep hid in the big barn, and one sheep had to have her neck stitched all the way around. The pasture wasn't happy at all that night; it cried in sorrow.

At another time a beautiful, curious, young lamb named George found a hole in the fence; the grass looked so much better to him on the other side. So he crawled through the hole. How could the young lamb know there was so much danger through the hole? How could the young lamb know there was so much danger lurking outside the safety of the happy pasture? A big dog was roaming and saw George. The other sheep inside the pasture saw the dog, and ran to the safety of the big barn as fast as they could.

The shepherd saw the sheep running; he could see they were terribly afraid. He quickly counted them and found one lamb missing. Then he heard the barking of the big dog. He ran as fast as he could to where the barking was coming from, but it was too late. George tried to make it back to the safety

Stories from the Shepherd's heart

of the pasture, but the big dog was much quicker than the little lamb. The dog made his attack just as the shepherd was arriving on the scene. The shepherd fearlessly drove off the dog, and gently lifted the wounded lamb to his arms.

The shepherd took George to the doctor of sheep. The news about George was not good. The bite went down to the bone. Muscles were torn. It was very serious; the cost would be very high to make little George well. The shepherd loved George. He was the firstborn that year. He was beautiful and strong, and always so curious. No cost would be too great if it would make George well...

Doesn't that remind you of our perfect Shepherd, Jesus, who saved us at the supremely high price? He saved us by giving up His own life – the highest price Jesus could pay – just for us.

The sheep doctor and the shepherd did all they humanly could do for George, but the shock and injury and pain and loneliness was more than the little lamb could bear, and he died.

It was many days before the rest of the flock at the sheep farm would leave the safety of the big barn. They had seen it happen and were afraid.

Dear children, always stay in the safety of God's happy pasture...do not willfully wander away. That old dog we call the devil, or Satan, is very real out there. Satan is roaming around waiting to pounce on God's lambs. He wants to inflict serious wounds on us; his utmost desire is to destroy our lives forever.

One day again, this world will be all new and clean and perfect. It will happen after Jesus comes back again. God is going to make a new heaven and a new earth. (Revelation 21:1). There will be no more sadness and no more tears. No one will be mean anymore. No more fighting, no more sin to ruin everything beautiful. God says something beautiful about that time in

Isaiah 11:6:
"The wolf will live with the lamb,
the leopard will lie down with the goat,
the calf and the lion and the yearling together;
and a little child will lead them."

Adoption

Little lambs have an adoption day every summer. The shepherd would love to keep every lamb which is born on the happy sheep farm, but the shepherd knows he could never properly take care of such a large flock. The pasture would become to small if too many sheep were grazing on it, so the shepherd has to have an adoption day for the lambs. Other families will have lambs to raise, and they will become shepherds of sheep. They too, will better understand the many Bible passages which compare people to sheep. The shepherd is delighted when his little lambs go to good homes.

Many of you who are reading this story are adopted. Most adoptions are made up of deep sadness and great joy. Many times the young birth mother just cannot give her baby a good home. Often, she is poor and alone, unable to properly feed or clothe or educate or care for her child. Because she had deep feelings of love for this child, she chose to not have an abortion; but rather, she carried her baby until the time of birth. Then she gave the baby up for adoption, giving another father and mother, who otherwise might never have a child, this baby to love and care for, and give a good, solid home to. The birth mother had much sadness and so did the childless couple, but now they have great joy.

There are other reasons for adoption too. Sometimes good parents are killed in wars or in accidents, and their children must be brought up by new parents.

Some children have very poor parents: parents who physically abuse their children, parents who have not met Jesus, parents who find comfort in drugs and alcohol. In extreme cases, these children must have a new home in which they, too, can flourish and experience kindness and love and enough to eat.

There are always many different reasons for adoption. The shepherd's family knows all about adoption.

First of all, Sarah came. She was from far away in Bangladesh. Her country was one of the poorest on the face of the earth. Her mother was poor and alone – an outcast from her Muslim religion. She was taken into a home for destitute women. Soon after her baby was born, she left – never to be heard from again. The mother knew she could not care for her baby girl. Many children in Bangladesh never live to see their fifth birthday because of the extreme poverty, illness, and hunger.

God had plans for Sarah. He wanted Sarah to be able to meet Jesus, so He made it possible for her to leave Bangladesh, and come to the United States and become the daughter of Christian parents. Sarah had to leave the only way of life she knew. She was frightened and cried a lot, but her deep sadness has turned to great joy, for now she is healthy and has a Christian family and she knows Jesus!

After Sarah came to the shepherd's family from Bangladesh, God, in His eternal wisdom, had a plan for two more little girls in India. He wanted them to be brought up in a Christian home where they, too, could meet Jesus. Laura and Carrie lived in great sadness. Their family was Hindu. Girl babies really aren't worth a whole lot in India. Boys are what the fathers want.

They lived in a family where their stepfather hated them. Carrie never had enough food, and for punishment, Laura was thrown into a fire. After their mother produced a son, the stepfather forced the mother to bring the girls to an orphanage. Laura and Carrie loved their mother, and their mother loved them. The grief for all of them was so enormous. The crying never stopped. God saw them in their deepest misery and made a way – impossible to man – for these little Hindu girls to come to the United States.

Now they have plenty of food, loving parents, a Christian home, an extended Christian family, and they have met Jesus. All day long, a smile is on their faces and a song on their lips. Their great sadness has turned to great joy.

The shepherd's family has children from India, Bangladesh, Korea, Russia, China and Chile – all these had to meet Jesus through adoption.

John 10:16 says it all so clearly: " I have other sheep that are not of this sheep pen. I must bring them also. They too will listen to my voice, and there will be one flock and one shepherd."

Back on the sheep farm, the day of adoption has come. The shepherd tries hard to have his lambs go to a good new shepherd. He reminds the new shepherds to learn all about sheep from the Bible. He loves to tell them how God compares people to sheep and lambs.

It is a sad day for the sheep farmer. By now he knows all the characteristics of the lambs. He has watched them skip and jump; some he has nursed back to life from near death. He knows good friends will be separated. Yet he knows it is for the good of the sheep; he cannot possibly care for the many lambs born on the sheep farm.

When the new owners come to pick up the lambs, the mother sheep seem to know what is going on; they become very nervous. The shepherd's heart becomes very heavy and aches for his sheep. After the new owners leave the farm with their lambs, the mother sheep cry and cry for their babies. The shepherd hears them all night long, crying in the pasture, and he sorrows with them.

The lambs, too, are very afraid when they get to their new home. They hardly eat or drink for a few days. They cry a lot for their mothers and old home. The new owners talk kindly to them and gently lead them to new pastures. Soon, they forget about their old home. They begin a new life in a new pasture and a new happy sheep farm. The children at the new home learn to care for the lambs, the same way God cares for them. Psalm 23 takes on a new meaning for them.

"The Lord is my Shepherd, I shall lack for nothing. He makes me lie down in green pastures, He leads me beside quiet waters, He restores my soul."

Do you know that all of us who know Jesus as our Savior are adopted children of God Almighty?

For us, too, there was a great sadness before we met Jesus. We were living in sin - miserable and unhappy. Then

Jesus came into our hearts. Our lives were changed and new meaning came into our daily lives. Like all the Sarahs and Lauras and Carries, we have a song on our lips and a smile on our face, because Jesus has made the change in our life!

Orphan Anne

I probably had the most compassion for Anne than any other lamb born. Anne is very special, and very close to the shepherd's heart.

It doesn't matter where Anne is or how far away – if she hears her shepherd call her name, she comes. She loves her shepherd very much and follows him.

She is also a very good mother, and every spring rewards the shepherd with one or two or even three lambs.

Anne was only a week old when her mother died suddenly of unknown causes. Anne cried and cried for her mother. The shepherd's heart ached for her. He gently picked her up – feeling her loneliness. He knew he would now be her substitute mother. She wasn't old enough to eat grass or hay, and hadn't learn to drink water yet. The shepherd prepared a special formula made of eggs, canned milk and cod liver oil. He put the milk in a baby bottle, and tried to coax Anne to drink the life-saving formula. At first, Anne refused to suck. The nipple on the baby bottle just wasn't like her mother. The shepherd was very patient, and finally Anne began to suck. The shepherd breathed a sigh of relief, and Anne's stomach felt much better. The Shepherd brought Anne a bottle every four hours and she was always waiting for it. She would nudge her shepherd, like a lamb does its mother. The shepherd made her a special place in the barn away from the other sheep so she could grow stronger.

Many days, the shepherd let her run on the lawn, hoping she would learn to eat grass. Instead, she would romp with the cats, walk with the ducks and follow the shepherd!

She even went to pre-school one day. The children were learning about sheep, and the teacher wanted a real sheep to come. The shepherd made sure she was nice and clean, and put a pretty red bow around her neck. The children were delighted, and even fed her a bottle. Anne loved the attention. She skipped and played with the children.

There was added excitement at the shepherd's home. Our last little lamb came to us from Guangzhou, China. Most likely her parents wanted a boy, and were disappointed a girl was born. They are only allowed one child, and most Chinese parents want that child to be a boy.

They brought their baby girl to a biscuit factory and laid her on the ground hoping someone would notice the little bundle. Someone did spot her, and brought her to the police station. The police, in turn, brought her to the orphanage. She was now an orphan, just like Anne. She had parents, but they abandoned her. The first six years of her life were spent in the orphanage. China called her a special needs child, maybe that's why she wasn't adopted sooner...maybe not. God knew all about her and He had a very special home waiting for her. The time wasn't right yet. Our son and

Stories from the Shepherd's heart

daughter-in-law were busy adopting from Siberia. They now had four children, two of which were adopted from Siberia. They were very happy with their four children. God must have been smiling, watching them, knowing their family wasn't complete. One day, out of the blue, the adoption agency called, stating that there was a little girl in China that would fit perfectly in their home! At first they felt they couldn't even consider it. Adoptions are very expensive, and they already had four children. They began getting signs that they had to get her. God kept urging them and wouldn't let them find peace. Finally, they gave it completely over to God and said, "God if it's your will for us to get her, You have to provide the funds. We do not have the money!" Well, God did provide. They ventured out in faith. Thus, they gave her the name "Hannah Faith". Hannah means "blessed of God." and "Hope". They chose Faith because they were venturing out with complete faith in God. Now Hannah knows Jesus!

The Shepherd's heart is sad – sad for all the orphans in the world – children of all ages who have no home. In Africa, little children see their parents killed and then are left all alone , crying and hungry. In Haiti, one of the poorest countries, children have no decent clothes to cover them up. Many have no clothes at all.

The shepherd is happy for the children rescued from the orphanages in his family, but what about all the rest who did not get adopted. Do we even hear their cries?

Could it be that someone reading my story could make room in their family for a destitute child? It isn't possible for everyone, but all of us can support those who leave the comforts of home to adopt, or start orphanages, in places where there would otherwise be no hope for the children.

My Shepherd, Jesus, is a father to the fatherless, but the children need someone to bring the Good News about Jesus, so they have hope and a future.

Jesus loves all the children of the world. He is not pleased to see children suffer. Children have a huge place in the heart of Jesus. In Matthew 18:3 Jesus says, "unless you change and become like little children, you will never enter the kingdom of heaven." It says again in Matthew 18:6, "But if anyone causes one of these little ones who believe in me to sin, it would be better for him to have a large millstone hung around his neck and to be drowned in the depths of the sea." In Matthew 19:14, Jesus said, "Let the little children come to me, and do not hinder them, for the kingdom of heaven belongs to such as these!"

This last verse makes me think about adoption and how important it is to bring a child into the household of faith. Mark 9:37 says "Whoever welcomes one of these little children in my name, welcomes me; and who ever welcomes me does not welcome me but the one who sent me."

Stories from the Shepherd's heart

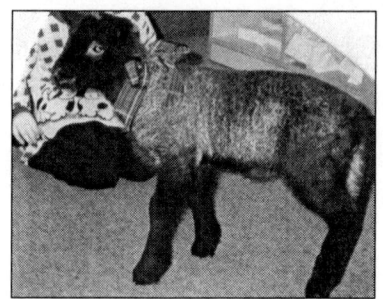

A Good Laugh on the Sheep Farm

When most people see a flock of sheep contentedly grazing in a pasture, they see a peaceful, pastoral scene. They love to stop and watch them, coaxing them to the fence with a handout.

Behind the scenes is a lot of hard, sometimes back-breaking work. It is espeically difficult in the wintertime, when the sheep are penned up inside. The pens the sheep live in have to be kept clean. It was the duty of the shepherd's youngest son to keep them that way.

One winter evening, he put off his chore until after supper. He backed the tractor and farm wagon through the doorway of the barn, and began shoveling away. Soon the wagon was heaping full, and since it was dark and rather late, he pulled the wagon a few hundred feet from the barn in between the sheep farm and the neighbor's place. The "neighbor's place" really was a car lot, situated in the middle of farm country. Being a Wednesday night, the car lot was open and towns-folk, with nothing better to do, were car shopping. The owner himself was a city person.

There was a gentle breeze blowing from the west to the east and in the breeze was the wonderful-smelling perfume from the farm wagon.

Everyone at the car lot noticed a strange aroma. "Gas fumes," someone offered, "It must be a gas leak somewhere".

The sheep were settling down to a long winter's nap. They were enjoying the good-smelling, fresh, dry straw.

The shepherd and his family had finished their hard day's work, bathed, and sunk into easy chairs to read and watch television.

Everyone jolted up! Sirens were coming from everywhere. They were stopping nearby. Someone shouted, "They're at the car lot!" Police cars, fire engines and an E-unit – came barreling in one by one they and came to a screeching halt. Men with flashlights in hand went around and around the building, inside and outside, checking out every possible thing. People were streaming to the car lot to see what could be wrong.

The men could not find the problem. The odor was strong, but where was it coming from?

One wise, country-bred fireman had an idea about what could be the problem; with flashlight in hand, followed his nose to a farm trailer, full of "leaking gas"!

One by one, the fire engines, police cars, E-unit, customers, and passersby left. What a good laugh they all had!

The shepherd's family walked home together, with sides aching from laughter. The sheep, unaware of what was happening, contentedly rested in the fresh straw.

Those sheep brought good humor and a good laugh.

Do you think our Good Shepherd sits in heaven and laughs at us. Sometimes?

I know God has a wonderful sense of humor – you can see it in His creation. You can see it especially in baby animals.

It is good for us to be happy and to have a good hearty laugh.

Proverbs 17:22 states, "A cheerful or merry heart is good medicine."

Shepherds and Sheep

As we have learned in all the "Good Shepherd" stories, sheep are wonderful animals. They all have different natures.

Some of their characteristics are timid: shy, curious, naughty, afraid, and bold. They all have one thing in common: and that is they are all helpless. They all need their earthly shepherd to lead and guide them.

Many things happen on a sheep farm. Some lambs are born sickly and weak; sheep are under the curse of sin and get sick. They have self-inflicted problems, such as wandering away and getting lost. Sheep cannot fight off enemies, such as dogs or wolves. They need their shepherd to protect them. They need their shepherd to provide them with a good pasture – with hay and grain and cool water and a place of safety.

I marvel at the pictures in the Bible of sheep and shepherds and people. Those who do not really understand sheep are often heard calling them "stupid". I feel that they mistake sheeps' helpless nature as a reason for calling them "dumb."

I just cannot help but believe that God very much loves the way of sheep, and that is why we, His people, are called "sheep."

Ezekiel 34:31 says, "You my sheep, the sheep of my pasture, are people, and I am your God, declares the Sovereign Lord."

It is such a beautiful picture. In fact, the entire chapter of Ezekiel talks about sheep and shepherds.

Our Good Shepherd is Jesus. We are sheep. But we people also have earthly shepherds, namely, our pastors. Like the shepherds of the sheep, the shepherds of the people have an enormous responsibility. They couldn't do a good job without the help of God, and without the Holy Spirit indwelling them. The Word of God must be preached in truth by them, and also lived by them.

They must spend hours in quiet study of God's Word, and have a total commitment to Christ. Preaching of the word is probably easy, compared to dealing with the sheep. It is easy to love the friendly, helpful, outgoing, generous, well-educated, motivated sheep; but a good shepherd is also called to love the lazy, shy, fault-finding, weak, wandering, lost sheep of the flock. The way a shepherd deals with these sheep determines how good a shepherd he is.

Ezekiel 34 talks about poor shepherds who do not care about problem sheep. Pastors know nothing about a 40-hour work week. Some nights a good pastor sees no sleep. He must tend to the sick, the dying, the problems, and the hurting.

Back on the sheep farm, there are many days the shepherd aches because of hard work. There are times that the

Stories from the Shepherd's heart

flock needs his care through the night hours. A good shepherd loves his sheep, regardless of the problems.

Praise be to God, there is comfort for all of us sheep and shepherds! God is ultimately in control of His flock and His church, and it will be cared for in spite of shortcomings and failures.

Ezekiel 34:15 and 16, "I myself will tend my sheep and have them lie down, declares the Sovereign Lord. I will search for the lost and bring back the strays. I will bind up the injured and strengthen the weak . . . I will shepherd the flock with justice."

Take time to Study God's Word, know the Shepherd, and feel the great love and compassion He has for you, His sheep.

The Sound of the Trumpet

It was a beautiful, sunny, Sunday morning in April. Before church, the shepherd's daughter went to check the sheep. Screams pierced the air – hysterical screams. The shepherd will never forget the horror of that morning. Noises came from the pasture like a low growl. The sights cannot be erased from memory, and are yet to awful to record on paper.

Four German shepherds were still at their ugly, vicious work . . . tearing apart the sheep. Bleeding sheep lay everywhere. Some were already dead, some barely alive. Terror gripped the shepherd. He quickly summoned help, and not even realizing his own danger, drove off the dogs. The neighbor, with a long range rifle, was able to shoot one fleeing dog.

Misery was everywhere. Anyone seeing, the sight or realizing how vulnerable a sheep is, would never allow their dogs to roam at will.

The veterinarian was called. Some of the sheep, still living, had to be put to sleep. Out of seven sheep, only two survived. One young ewe had her neck stitched halfway around her head; another older ewe had wisely hidden in the barn and was never touched.

The shepherd sees another picture:

God's sheep are suffering all over the world. Christians in a number of countries are routinely arrested and thrown into jail, just for practicing their faith.

Many Southern Sudanese Christians, who refuse to yield and submit to the laws of Islam have been put to death.

Burma is a country where there are Christian Karen and Karenni tribes. Many who are Christians are persecuted and tortured, and their churches have been burned. All this happens because they seek to worship God who is unrecognized by the Buddhist regime.

Azerbaijan, an Islamic nation of seven million, has an explicit policy of ethnic cleansing against Armenian Christians.

Persecution against Chinese Catholics and evangelicals continues. Chinese law forbids private Christian worship, or attendance at non-state sanctioned churches.

There is a determined persecution against Christians in Saudi Arabia.

The list goes on. There is war and bloodshed in Russia, Bosnia, Iran, Pakistan, India, and North Korea.

Those places are far away. At least in the United States, things are different, right? Wrong!

Our children cannot pray in school, because one woman said it wasn't constitutional. One person, in an entire town of Bloomingdale, said a picture of Christ hanging on a school wall offended him, and it had to be removed. Evolution can be taught as fact, but the true story of creation with God as the

Creator cannot even be taught as a theory. Religious songs cannot be sung at a Christmas program at school.

What about God's lambs, yet unborn, torn apart by the abortionist? What about states making laws saying it is okay to kill the elderly or impaired, and calling it "mercy killing."

Let's not ignore the signs of the earth. Earthquakes, floods, hurricanes, tornadoes, mudslides, are increasing worldwide in frequency and magnitude.

All of creation is moaning and crying out, "Lord, how long?"

Listen to a few words from our Good Shepherd as He talked about these very things.

In Matthew 24 He said,

Nation will rise up against nation, kingdom against kingdom.

Verse 9: "Then you will be handed over to be persecuted and put to death, and you will be hated by all nations because of me. Many will turn away from the faith and will betray and hate each other, and many false prophets will appear and deceive many people. Because of the increase of wickedness, the love of most will grow cold, but he who stands firm to the end will be saved."

Verse 21: There will be great distress, unequaled from the beginning of the world until now – never to be equaled again.

Verse 42 states: Keep watch, because you do not know on what day your Lord will come.

Verse 44 says: You must be ready because the Son of Man will come at an hour you do not expect Him.

Then let's go back to verse 30 and praise the Lord for what we read there: "The sign of the Son of Man will appear in the sky, and all the nations of the earth will mourn. They will see the Son of Man coming on the clouds of the sky, with power and great glory. And He will send His angels with a loud trumpet call, and they will gather His elect from the four winds, from one end of the heavens to the other."

    Oh church, sheep of the Good Shepherd, lift up your heads – redemption draweth nigh!

Lessons from the Good Shepherd

A long time ago, when I was a young wife with little children, Harold surprised me one day by saying, "You know, I think that we ought to get a couple lambs for the kids!" He had lambs when he was a boy and always liked them, and he also figured it would teach the kids responsibility.

Little did either one of us realize that the sheep and lambs would be such an important part of my journey! You see, we are on a journey through life, on a path or road leading us to a much better place. Circumstances through life should keep us straight on the path headed for heaven! For me, God has used sheep to teach me so many lessons.

Our first sheep, Mary, came to us as just a little lamb. She was scared to death. She had been taken from her mother and everything she was familiar with. Adoption lesson: We're all adopted by God to be His sons and daughters because of what Jesus has done for us. Adoption is both sad and joyful. Our granddaughter Sarah's mother was alone and destitute living in Bangladesh where many children never see their 5th birthday. She knew she didn't have the where-with-all to care

Stories from the Shepherd's heart

for a baby – and what future would she have? She reluctantly gave her up for adoption. Granddaughters Laura and Carrie's mother, in heavy sobs, brought her little girls to the orphanage. In India, girls are not important. Her husband didn't want the girls, especially after a baby boy was born. He said the girls had to go. Grandson Nikolas was born prematurely. His mother abandoned him at the hospital; she couldn't care for him. Russia is poor beyond what we can imagine.

Granddaughter Ekaterina's mother lived in a very small apartment. She looked much older than her actual years due to a hard life in Siberia. She was very poor. She could not possibly raise another child.

With tears streaming down her face, she released Ekaterina for adoption. Adoption brings joy. These children find joy coming to a country like America; and they bring joy to their adopted parents and grandparents. They belong, they have a family and are part of the family of God.

Mary the ewe lamb settled down and loved the children and her new home. Harold soon added a little white ram. I knew absolutely nothing about sheep, coming from town, so I had to read books to learn how to care for them.

They say that shepherds were lowly people, and yet when I read about shepherds in the Bible I would desire to be one of them! I think that as the shepherds sat out in the fields with their sheep, they must have felt very near to God. David took a negative situation and used his time in a positive way, because it was while he was alone watching sheep that he wrote so many psalms. It also was there that David felt God's presence with him when he had to kill the wild animals that intended to harm the sheep. And really, wouldn't it have been great to be a shepherd the night that Jesus was born and to be able to see and hear the angels? I love how the shepherds rushed to the manger and worshiped the new born king. Those "lowly" shepherds were so excited that they just couldn't help telling everyone that they met on their way back to the sheep!

As the years passed our sheep produced many young. We soon had a small flock, but never kept more than twelve at a time.

Verses from the Bible began to have new meaning to me. Verses that I had skipped over before, I now underlined and pondered. The whole chapter of Ezekiel 34, a chapter of shepherds and sheep (read it sometime), talks about earthly shepherds compared to the Good Shepherd. I love the last verse, Ezekiel 34:31. It says, "You my sheep, the sheep of my pasture, are people, and I am your God, declares the Sovereign Lord!"

At sometime in my journey in life, I began to know and love all of the references in the Bible about sheep and about how God compares us to sheep. In my mind, I think God saw something special about sheep, and I have to pay close attention to what He has to say about me, His sheep. After all, I am on a journey, and I have to stay on the right road to reach my destination.

Lambs are so small, so weak and so helpless. They need their shepherd at birth to warm them up and get them on their feet. How they love to snuggle up to the shepherd. They put their little faces up close to my face, like babies. Like infants they grow – little children playing, running, laughing – little lambs running, jumping, and carefree. If they wander too far from their mother, she calls out to them and they skip back to her. As night falls, Mother tucks her little children into bed. Isaiah 40:11 says, "He tends His flock like a shepherd; He gathers the lambs in His arms and carries them close to His heart; He gently leads those that have young."

Matthew 19:14 says "...Let the little children come to me, and do not hinder them, for the kingdom of heaven belongs to such as these." In my journey, I had to learn such a hard lesson. Sometimes little lambs die for one reason or another. When sin came into the world, death came along with it. Little children can die, too. Rachel (meaning ewe lamb, patient while suffering) was taken home to be with the Lord at the tender age of seven; she was so beautiful, so full of life, so much potential. But she knew and loved her Shepherd and she is safe in His arms, waiting for us to be done with our journey. Parents, the most important thing that you can do is to make sure your children know all about the Good Shepherd.

I imagine sheep could survive without a shepherd for a short time, provided there was a good pasture for food and still waters for them to drink, but alas there are always predators. If ever the shepherd is needed it's when the predators are prowling. In our area, the predators are dogs and coyotes. Sheep where not created to defend themselves. I still remember with much sadness a night when, while the family was sleeping, four German Shepherds came and attacked. How horrible! The picture is still so vivid in my mind, dead and dying sheep. The tears flowed and it was hard to be comforted because we were miserable shepherds. But I know from the Bible that God is the Good Shepherd. God does not sleep. He watches over me day and night. God gives me in His Word what I need to know to be able to fight my predator, the devil;

and when I am in immediate danger, God sends His angels to protect me. Jesus had compassion on the crowds "because they were harassed and helpless, like sheep without a shepherd." (Matthew 9:36)

Sheep also get lost. They never forget where that hole is in the fence. One time we had a gate that didn't fasten well and until we figured out the problem, the sheep managed to open that gate every day and find freedom. But a secure gate doesn't necessarily ensure safety for the sheep. If they want to escape badly enough they can jump fences as easily as a deer. Our sheep never wandered far, but one Sunday afternoon, we had a large flock of sheep wander over. Their pasture was over two miles away! Their shepherd had to come and get them, of course, given that, on their own, they would keep wandering and never find their way home. That reminds of the parable of the lost sheep in Matthew 18: 12-13. I can just visualize the shepherd, scratched and bleeding, carrying that sheep over his shoulders with a great big smile on his face. That's what Jesus does for us!

Sad to say, the sheep grow old. They get arthritis just as we do. It's hard for them to get up. They need special love and care. They can no longer keep up with the flock. They sleep often. Yet the shepherd still cares. After all, they are good sheep. He has many good memories of better days.

Lord, you want me to go and help your aged sheep at the nursing home? I wasn't sure I could do that! I learned another lesson. These are beautiful people, God's old sheep of the flock, people with a beautiful journey of their own to talk about. They are people who lived through depression, war, sickness, poverty and trials of every imaginable kind, and yet they testify as to how the Good Shepherd was with them all the way on their journey. For them, the journey is nearing its end.

You have probably heard it said that sheep are dumb. Well, I have to submit to you that there is one way in which I am sure sheep can be smarter than people. You see, the sheep know the shepherd's voice. I love John 10:3, "He calls His own sheep by name and leads them out. When he has brought out all His own, he goes on ahead of them, and His sheep follow Him because they know His voice." John 10:14 says, "I am the good shepherd; I know my sheep and my sheep know me." And then regarding sheep in John 10:5, "they will never follow a stranger; in fact, they will run from him because they do not recognize a stranger's voice." In the sheep world, I can testify to this truth. No mater how far away the sheep are, when I call they come running to me. They know my voice. But if you tried the same thing, they would run from you. How sad it is that we don't always hear our Good Shepherd calling to us. He knows every one of us by name. Isn't it sad to think that we would chose to follow someone or something other than our Good Shepherd? Another lesson on my journey: sheep have to follow the Good Shepherd in order to stay on the right road going in the right direction!

Well, Harold and I are getting older. We know someday we no longer will be able to keep the sheep. When we have to give them up I will miss them, but will always be grateful for the lessons taught on our very important journey through this life.

Stories from the Shepherd's heart